ON THE
WING

ON THE WING

American Birds in Migration

CAROL LERNER

HarperCollinsPublishers

For Andrea

On the Wing
Copyright © 2001 by Carol Lerner
Printed in Hong Kong. All rights reserved.
www.harperchildrens.com

Library of Congress Cataloging-in-Publication Data
Lerner, Carol.
   On the wing : American birds in migration / Carol Lerner.
      p.   cm.
   ISBN 0-688-16649-0 — ISBN 0-688-16650-4 (lib. bdg.)
   1. Birds—Migration—North America—Juvenile literature.
   [1. Birds—Migration.]   I. Title.
QL698.9 L47   2001   00-38831
598.156'8'0973—dc21   CIP
                                                              AC

2   3   4   5   6   7   8   9   10
❖
First Edition

CONTENTS

WHY BIRDS MIGRATE

All over the world millions of birds set off on long, perilous migrations each year. Bird migration is a regular mass movement. Birds fly from winter homes to summer nesting areas in spring and make the return trip in fall.

If you follow these vast movements of wildlife, you can witness some of the great spectacles of the natural world. Even before the end of winter, flocks of blackbirds begin streaming into northern wetlands to feed and to claim nesting territories. More species return in the early days of spring—ducks, killdeers, woodcocks, phoebes, and kinglets. As spring advances, the woodlands start to fill as more and more birds join the procession. Flocks of thousands swarm into wetland refuges to feed and rest before continuing the journey.

Fall ushers in the second half of the spectacle. Now many of the migrants are less colorful. The bright feathers that they wore in the mating season have been replaced by duller ones. And their numbers are greater; offspring that were born during the summer months are ready to join their parents on the return trip. About five billion land birds from five hundred different species leave their North American nesting areas to spend the winter farther south.

These migration journeys are dangerous. The birds must travel through unfamiliar territory and are always at the mercy of unseen predators. Changing weather is another threat. A sudden storm can blow small birds off course. An unexpected cold snap that keeps insects in winter hibernation can mean starvation, for most birds must feed as they travel.

Some birds avoid the hazards of migration by staying in one place all year. By remaining behind, they can claim the best nesting areas before the migrants return next spring. Stay-at-homes usually lay their first set of eggs earlier in the spring and are able to raise more young than migrants coming to the same area.

But these birds also pay a price for remaining in a cold climate. Many kinds of food—active insects and fresh fruits, for example—are absent in winter. Seeds may become buried under heavy snow or ice. Mice and other small mammals—food for birds of prey—stay hidden in their nests in extreme cold.

At the same time that food is in short supply, the need for it is greater than ever. Although birds are very well insulated from the cold by their feathers, like all warm-blooded animals they need more food in winter just to keep up their body temperatures. And for birds that are active during the day, the short hours of sunlight mean less time to search for food. If they eat too little, they will freeze during the long winter nights.

By braving the long journey, migrants enjoy a more comfortable winter home. In a milder climate they need less food, and it is easier to find. By living in two different places, they can also eat a more varied diet over the course of the year. They may be better nourished than birds that never move.

Yet migrants stopping off in Texas, Mexico, or Central America enter territories that already have their own bird populations, and winter quarters are often crowded. When it is again time to nest and raise a new generation, the need for food will skyrocket, straining the local resources. So migrant species take to the air again, heading toward the vast landscapes of Canada and the northern United States with their plentiful space and food.

◆　◆　◆

If you are like most people, you probably thought that migration is a simple retreat from winter, an annual move from the colder parts of North America to the warmer areas in the south. In fact, migrating birds show a wide variety of behaviors, following schedules and routes that have been used by members of their species over the generations.

On the Wing looks at the main migration patterns of American birds as well as at some variations. Each kind of migratory habit this book discusses is illustrated using one or more species as examples. A map shows their summer and winter ranges. The summer range—the area where the bird may be seen during the summer season—is shown in pink. The winter range is in blue. Areas where a species lives year-round are in purple.

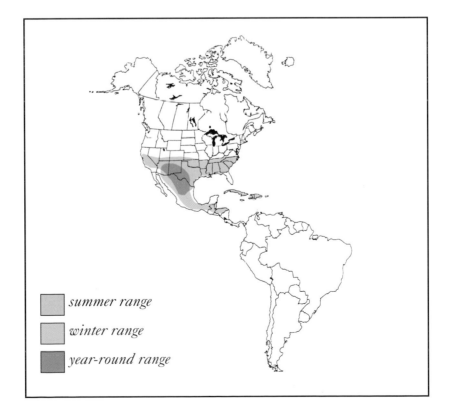

□ *summer range*

□ *winter range*

■ *year-round range*

PARTIAL MIGRATION

If you live in the north, the first robin you see in the new year is a sign of spring. But like many species, the robin is a migrant in only part of its range. In the southern states robins are common all year long.

Most robins that spend the nesting season in the north migrate to the southern United States, Mexico, or the Caribbean islands for the winter. They join the year-round robins of those places, forming large winter flocks. This kind of migratory pattern, in which some birds move for the winter and others do not, is called partial migration.

The migration pattern of robins is relatively simple. The movements of some other partial migrants are more complicated. In some species one part of the same population—sometimes males or females, sometimes parents or their offspring—has a different migration pattern.

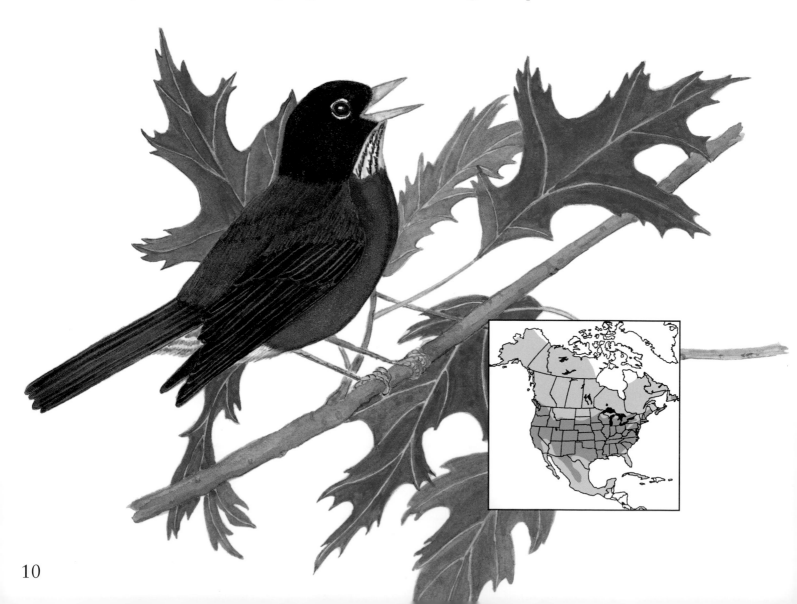

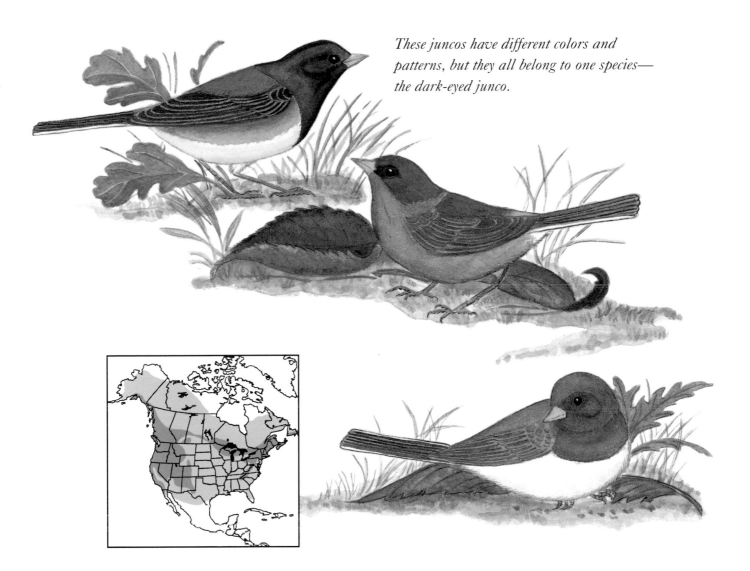

These juncos have different colors and patterns, but they all belong to one species— the dark-eyed junco.

Female dark-eyed juncos, for example, migrate farther than the males do. In other species young birds make longer migrations than the older birds.

Scientists suggest explanations for these differing patterns. In the case of juncos, staying closer to the northern nesting grounds gives the males a better chance to claim good territory in the spring. In places where winter food is scarce, birds that are older and stronger save resources for themselves by driving away the younger and weaker ones.

How the Geography of North America Influences Migration Routes

When ducks, geese, and many smaller birds move up or down the continent, they follow four broad routes, or flyways. They begin the fall migration from nesting areas that are spread across Canada and the northern United States, but their paths narrow as they move southward and follow the great natural landmarks of North America. The Atlantic and Pacific

The North American Flyways

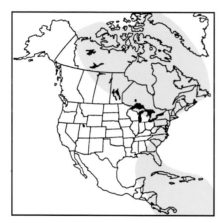

Atlantic flyway

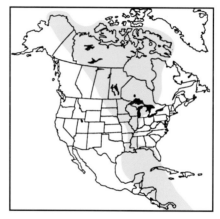

Mississippi flyway

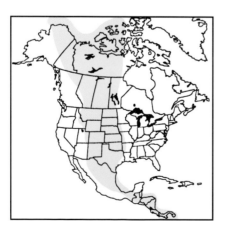

Central flyway

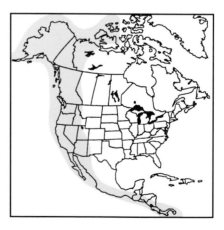

Pacific flyway

coastlines, the Mississippi River valley, and the major mountain chains—
the Sierras, Rockies, and Appalachians—all lead in a north-south direction.
These landmarks make it easier for birds to stay on course.

Differences in temperature between land and ocean create breezes
that provide tailwinds and give an extra lift to broad-winged coastal travelers. Soaring birds use rising air currents to glide along the mountain
chains (see pages 32–33). Ocean coastlines and the Mississippi River also
offer rich supplies of food as well as many resting places along the route.

MIGRATING WITHIN NORTH AMERICA

The main wintering areas for migrants from the United States and Canada are Mexico, Central America, and the Caribbean islands. About half of these birds go no farther south than Mexico and the West Indies.

But with millions of birds pouring into an area about one-eighth the size of their nesting grounds, how can the land provide enough room and food for them all? Especially since these places already have their own populations of year-round birds.

To begin with, the migrants need less food now than they did in the summer when they were laying eggs, feeding the young, and growing new feathers. Even so, the visiting birds still need to eat.

There are a number of solutions to this problem. Some birds arrive in the south during the season of plenty, when there is enough food for all. Other migrants go from place to place, searching out new areas whenever the local food supply is used up. Still others settle in places that are used very little by resident birds. In some areas the migrants are so numerous that they set up territories and dominate the resident birds.

Some migrants seem more at home in their wintering areas than on their nesting grounds. Tanagers are a large family of brightly colored Latin American birds. The name tanagers was given to them by the Tupi Indians of the Amazon, who call them *tangarás*. Most tanagers live in the dense forests of Central and South America, where as many as forty different species are found in one place. The family contains over two hundred and forty different species, but only four of them enter the United States to nest.

One of these four species is the western tanager. Western tanagers spend the warm months in the mountain forests of western Canada and the United States, feeding on insects in spring and early summer. Later in the season they eat berries and other fruits. In fall most migrate to the highlands of Mexico and Central America.

Preparing for Migration

As the time for spring migration draws near, birds undergo several changes. One change, the development of the sexual organs, prepares them for mating and reproduction.

Other physical changes prepare birds for the journey itself. Birds eat more before both spring and fall migrations, feeding almost constantly. The weight gain is stored as a layer of fat just beneath the skin. Fat is a very efficient fuel for the long trip. A tiny bird weighing only half an ounce (fifteen grams) can fly over 125 miles (200 kilometers) on one-thirtieth of an ounce (one gram) of fat.

The amount of weight a bird gains depends on the length of the journey ahead. Birds flying a few hundred miles may add another 13 to 25 percent to their body weights. But long-distance migrants can put on 50 to 100 percent more weight.

In addition to these physical changes, birds show a change in behavior called migratory restlessness. Caged migratory birds try to fly away, fluttering in the direction of their migratory route. Wild birds respond by actually starting off on their journeys.

All these preparations are triggered by a change in the hormones within the bird's body. Hormones are chemical substances that control and regulate body processes. They are released by organs called glands.

The hormone change is in response to two cues—one from outside and one from within. The first is day length, the lengthening period of daylight in spring and its shortening in fall.

The second cue is an internal clock that follows the cycle of the seasons. Evidence that birds respond to an internal clock comes from experiments with several species. Captive birds that were kept in artificial light on an unchanging schedule (twelve hours of light, twelve of darkness) still responded to the seasons as they would in the wild: They gained weight, showed migratory restlessness, and mated.

To demonstrate migratory restlessness, scientists place a bird in a funnel-shaped cage covered by a screen.

When the bird is ready to migrate, it strikes the side of the cage again and again, trying to fly away.

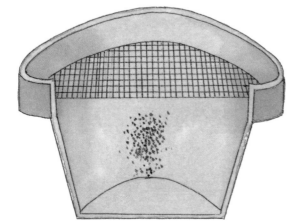

Its claws leave marks on paper that lines the cage. The marks show the direction in which the bird intended to fly.

CROSSING THE EQUATOR

While many fall migrants swarm into Mexico, Central America, or the West Indies, a small number of species go on to the South American continent. Only a few of these continue across the equator.

The winter home of the chimney swift was one of the last migratory destinations to be discovered. More than 375,000 swifts had been banded (see page 44), but not a single band had ever been returned. Finally, in 1944, Indian hunters brought in thirteen bands from birds that they had killed in northeastern Peru. The birds had been banded in Tennessee, Illinois, Connecticut, Alabama, Georgia, and Ontario.

Chimney swifts belong to the swift family, fast-flying acrobats that spend all their waking hours in the air. These birds eat on the wing, catching flying insects in their wide mouths. They even drink, bathe, and collect nesting materials while in flight. To land on flat ground is actually dangerous. Their legs are small and weak, so it is hard for them to take off from a horizontal surface.

But swifts have strong claws. They rest by clinging to vertical surfaces and propping their bodies with their short, spine-tipped tails. At one time chimney swifts flew into hollow trees to rest and make their nests. They are called chimney swifts because today they often use chimneys as a substitute for dead trees.

At sundown flocks of migrating swifts circle in the sky above a large chimney or air shaft. Finally they drop down into the opening to rest for the night.

Finding the Way

How do migrating birds find their way to their winter areas and back again to the nesting grounds? Some young birds—such as geese, swans, and many seabirds—migrate from their place of birth as part of a family group and so are introduced to the route by their parents. To the degree that birds follow major landmarks (see page 12), young birds can learn to recognize these features. But some migrations take birds over seas and oceans, where there are no physical features that can guide them in future journeys.

And what of young birds making their first journey without adults? Herring gulls and American golden plovers, for example, set off on their initial fall migration without experienced guides.

Experiments have shown that birds can use a variety of cues to find the right direction. During daytime travel, the sun offers a way to determine direction. Viewed from the United States or Canada, the sun is always due south at noon. But since the sun appears to move through the sky in the course of the day, it isn't possible to tell directions from its position without knowing the time of day. Once you know the time, you can make allowance for the sun's changing position and calculate where it would be at noon. Scientists believe that birds have a kind of internal clock that allows them to use the sun as a compass.

Experiments show that it is possible to confuse a bird's sense of direction by resetting its internal clock. Homing pigeons were kept in artificial light conditions for several days. The lights went on six hours before sunrise and went off six hours before sunset. When the pigeons were released at nine in the morning, their internal clocks told them it was three in the afternoon. Judging directions by what they believed was the position of the sun in the afternoon, they flew off in the wrong direction.

When birds fly at night and the sun can give no guidance, they can use the polestar and the surrounding constellations to find their way. The polestar, also called Polaris or the North Star, is a fixed point in the night sky of the Northern Hemisphere. It stands still while nearby constellations appear to circle it.

How do birds find their way when clouds hide the sun or stars? One clue to this mystery came in the late 1970s, when tiny bits of magnetite were found in the heads of homing pigeons. Magnetite, or lodestone, is a kind of iron ore that can be used like the needle on a compass to find directions. If a bar of magnetite is hung by a thread so it can move freely, one end always points to the north. Sailors used lodestones as far back as the Middle Ages to find their way at sea. The discovery of magnetite within birds' bodies suggests that they may have a built-in magnetic compass.

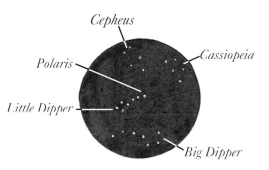

To show that birds use the stars as a compass, scientists place a bird in a funnel-shaped cage covered by a screen.

A picture of the northern sky is shown on the ceiling. The bird tries to fly in the direction of its migratory path.

When Polaris and some of its nearby constellations are removed, the bird still flies in the correct direction.

But when all the stars are removed, the bird is confused and flutters in all directions.

Although homing pigeons usually use the sun as their compass, they have shown that they could still find the way home on cloudy days when the sun is invisible. Their use of a magnetic compass was demonstrated in this experiment: Tiny magnets were placed on the pigeons' bodies. The magnets interfered with their ability to sense the earth's magnetic pull, and the birds lost their way.

Some scientists think that birds also use certain smells and sounds for guidance. There are still many unanswered questions about how birds receive information and use it to navigate.

ARCTIC NESTERS

The Arctic tundra of North America stretches across the continent from Alaska to Labrador in northern Canada. On this barren plain the trees are dwarfs, and no plant grows taller than eighteen inches (forty-six centimeters). For most of the year the land is snowbound and frozen.

By June the tundra has begun to thaw. Scattered ponds of melted water dot the plain, insects stir out of winter dormancy, grasses and sedges turn the earth green, and the trees and shrubs are tipped with new buds. With the long hours of daylight—twenty or more in every twenty-four—the plants grow rapidly and the insect population multiplies.

During the short Arctic summer, the explosion of plant and animal food provides a feast for wildlife. Although few species of birds live year-round in this bleak land, huge flocks of waterfowl and shorebirds come here to nest and raise their young. With little competition from resident

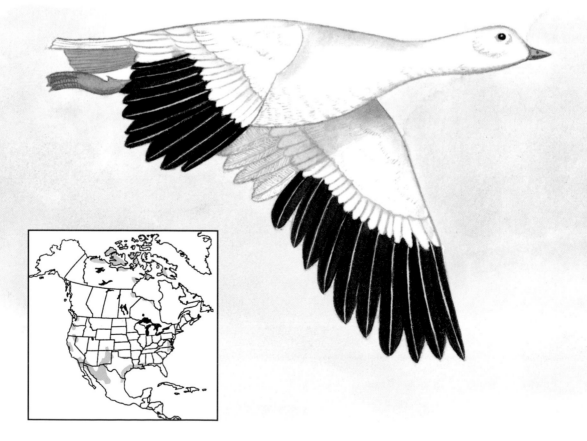

animals and few predators, the tundra is an ideal nursery.

Among these migrants is the snow goose, probably the most numerous species of goose in North America. More than two million fly to Arctic Canada in June. They come in mass flights and form nesting colonies of many thousand birds. Since the ground is still half-frozen, they must arrive with enough extra fat on their bodies (see page 16) to keep themselves nourished for the first week or two.

Because the Arctic summer is brief, there is no time to waste. Within three months the young and adults must be ready for the return flight. Snow geese, which form lifelong pairs, have already mated by the time they reach the nesting grounds. Upon arrival each pair stakes out its territory within the colony and begins nest building. The young hatch out about three weeks after eggs are laid. By late August or early September the adults have shed their old worn feathers and grown new ones, the young are strong enough to fly, and the families take off for migration. Their main wintering grounds are in California, Texas, and Mexico.

Nonstop Flights and Stopovers

Some birds follow migratory routes that are truly tests of endurance. The red knot, a large beach shorebird, makes one of the longest journeys of any bird in the Western Hemisphere. After nesting in the Arctic during the spring and summer, red knots head south. Some winter off the Atlantic or California coasts, but another part of the population flies all the way to the southern tip of South America. Before migrating, red knots add 40 to 50 percent to their body weights (see page 16). With this fuel load they can fly 1,850 miles (3,000 kilometers) without stopping.

ruby-throated hummingbird

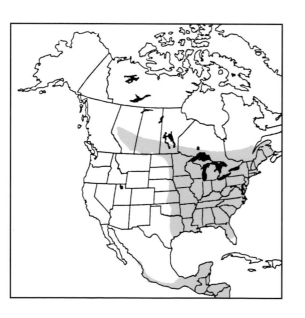

Even more remarkable are the nonstop flights of some small birds that travel over open water. Unable to stop and rest, they must fly until they reach the far shore. Some ruby-throated hummingbirds—a species that may weigh as little as one-tenth of an ounce (2.6 grams)—fly nonstop for five hundred miles (eight hundred kilometers) across the Gulf of Mexico.

Such nonstop flights are exceptions, however. Most birds make frequent layovers along the way to rest and feed. They avoid long water crossings. Birds traveling to the tropics fly over Mexico and Central America or else hop from island to island across the Caribbean.

Songbirds do not usually arrive in huge numbers at rest sites along the route, but larger birds, such as ducks, geese, and shorebirds, do. One important stopover site, or staging area, is the Platte River in Nebraska. It attracts five to nine million ducks and geese each spring. Perhaps its most impressive visitors are the sandhill cranes. About half a million of these birds—four-fifths of all the sandhill cranes in North America—gather here every year.

Although the crane weighs only seven to eight pounds (less than four kilograms), it stands over three feet (one meter) tall and has a wingspread of six or seven feet (two meters). Migratory cranes spend winter in Mexico and the southwestern United States. They arrive at the Platte from late February to early March. By day they feed in fields and meadows, eating waste grain, insects, crayfish, snails, and earthworms. At night they gather in the shallows of the river, where they are safe from prowling predators.

After six weeks of feeding, the cranes have added a pound (half a kilogram) of fat to their lanky bodies. By early April most flocks take off for nesting areas in Siberia, Alaska, and Canada.

sandhill crane

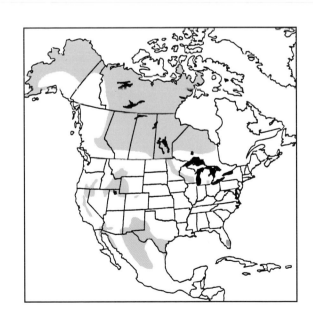

THE MIGRANTS OF SOUTH AMERICA

One day around March 21 the sun passes over the equator and appears to start moving northward. On that date the day and the night are of equal length. In the Northern Hemisphere that day, which is called the spring equinox, signals the beginning of longer daylight hours and the approach of summer. For those living in the southern half of the globe, it brings shorter days and the coming of fall.

In the lower portions of South America some birds begin to head north in March to spend their winter in warmer areas nearer the equator. Among these migrants is the vermillion flycatcher.

Flycatchers are a large family of South American birds. Of the 375 or so species in this family, only about a tenth ever come as far north as the United States. As their name suggests, many flycatchers feed by darting from perches and snatching up insects in midair.

Most flycatchers are plain, with brown, gray, or olive green feathers. The vermillion flycatcher is an exception. The male is bright red, and the female is grayish brown with a hint of bright color on her flanks.

Vermillion flycatchers are a widespread species. Some live in the southwestern United States, in Central America, and in northern South America.

Another population of these birds nests on the pampas, the open grassy plains, of central and southern South America. In March, at the end of their nesting season, they migrate as far north as the Amazon River basin, where they spend their winter in clearings, in fields with scattered trees, or along rivers and streams.

The Vanishing Forests

In recent decades bird-watchers in eastern North America realized that they were seeing fewer forest birds. Since many of these birds are long-distance migrants that spend the winter in Mexico and Central America, scientists looked to Latin America to explain the decline.

They knew that the rain forest homes of many birds are being destroyed. To feed growing populations in Latin America, great sections of tropical forests are being cleared for farming. These forestlands are not very fertile, and after a year or two of cultivation the soils lose their nutrients. In days past farmers then moved on to new areas, and in time new trees grew on the abandoned farmland. Some kinds of birds returned, though not the species that make their homes in old forests.

But farming practices are changing. With the increasing use of fertilizers, more cleared lands now become permanent cornfields or pastures for cattle. Very few kinds of birds live in agricultural fields.

The shrinking Latin American rain forests are only one side of the problem. The other lies in the forests of eastern North America, where so many migrants nest. Although the total number of wooded acres is still large, most of the forests themselves are small. Agriculture, housing developments, roads, and power lines have broken them into smaller and smaller units.

grackle and crow (left top and bottom)
blue jay and cowbird (right top and bottom)

This affects forest-nesting birds because any break in the solid forest is an entryway for nest raiders. Raccoons, blue jays, crows, and grackles seldom bother birds in the deep woods, but they destroy eggs in nests on the forest edge. Cowbirds live in open areas but invade the edges of woodlands. They remove the eggs of other birds and replace them with their own. Some species of birds nesting in these fragmented forests are declining in numbers because so few of their young survive.

As forests shrink, conservationists on both continents are working to protect bird habitats. The survival of many long-distance migrants will depend on their efforts.

EAST-WEST MIGRATION

Most migrant birds in the Northern Hemisphere fly south after the nesting season. But some find comfortable winter homes without leaving the cold North.

In North America white-winged scoters raise their young on nesting grounds in western Canada and Alaska. They live near ponds and lakes, feeding on crayfish and other small shellfish as well as insects, fish, and plants.

In fall most of them head east or west to the oceans. About 60 percent fly to the Atlantic coast; the rest go to the Pacific.

Scoters prefer cold water. They spend the winter a mile (1.6 kilometers) or so off the mainland in water that averages about fifty-six degrees Fahrenheit (thirteen degrees centigrade).

Scoters are diving ducks with webbed feet and powerful wing muscles for swimming underwater. They can remain below the surface for a full minute while searching for food. They may dive forty feet (twelve meters) deep to harvest shellfish from the ocean floor. Then they swallow the food whole, shell and all! Mussels over two and a half inches (six and a half centimeters) long have been found inside scoters. Some of the shells they swallow are so hard they can only be cracked with a hammer.

The scoter can digest this rock-hard food because, like all birds, it has a gizzard. This is a section of a bird's stomach made of powerful muscles with tough ridges on its inside wall. The gizzard does the same job as a mammal's strong jaws and teeth. It reduces hard food to small particles that the animal can then digest.

Flight Patterns

All birds flap their wings, but they all don't fly in the same way. The pattern of flight depends upon the weight of the bird and the size and shape of its wings.

Ducks and geese are heavy birds with narrow, pointed wings. Their strong breast muscles supply the power they need to move their wings

goose

and keep their bodies airborne. Except when landing, they flap their wings continually as they fly. Nonstop wing flapping takes a lot of energy, so these birds must pause along the migration route to rest and feed.

In contrast, birds that soar on outstretched wings use about one-twentieth of the energy needed for wing flapping. Eagles, vultures, and some hawks are among the soarers.

These birds spread their long, broad wings to catch rising hot air currents called thermals. As the sun heats the earth, the air at ground level is warmed. Warm air is lighter than the cold air above it, so it creates rising currents of air. The birds fly to the bottom of a thermal and gain height as they circle it. When the thermal weakens, they glide to the bottom of the next thermal and repeat the process. Soaring takes

hawk

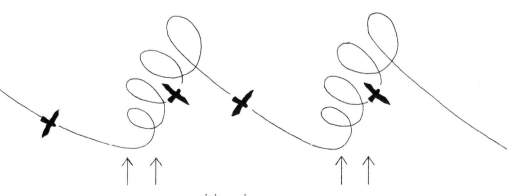

rising air currents

so little energy that a Swainson's hawk, an excellent soarer, can fly from New Mexico to Argentina without feeding along the way.

Warblers, thrushes, and other small birds have short, rounded wings that are not good for gliding. Their migration flying follows a pattern called bounding flight: The birds flap for a short period of time, then fold their wings and coast down.

Herons, crows, some wood-

thrush

flapping   *coasting*   *flapping*   *coasting*

peckers, and many other large birds have wings that are big enough to save some energy by gliding. They have a zigzag flight that combines flapping and gliding. They flap to gain height and speed, glide down, and then start the flapping sequence again.

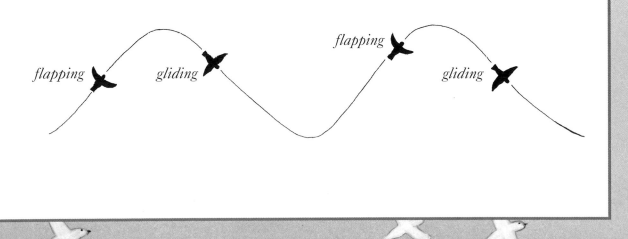

flapping   *gliding*   *flapping*   *gliding*

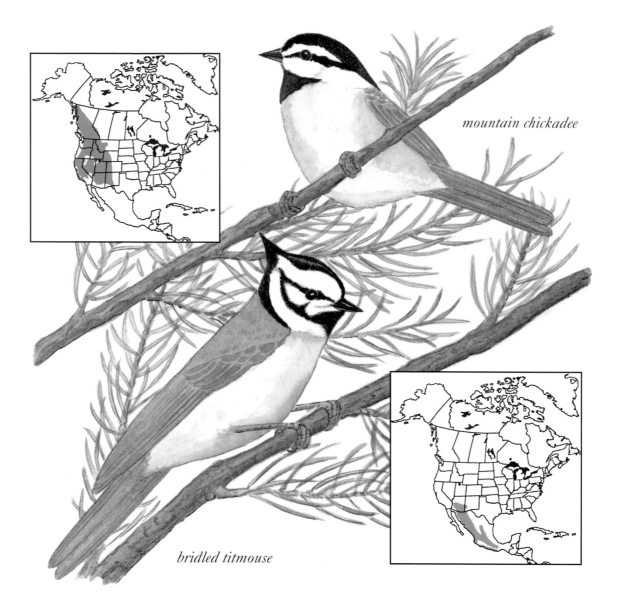

mountain chickadee

bridled titmouse

UP AND DOWN
THE MOUNTAIN

Many birds that live in the mountains make short seasonal migrations up and down the slopes. The journey may take them only 1,000 feet (305 meters), but in the mountains even a small change in elevation can mean a big difference in climate. By leaving the heights, the birds escape the most severe conditions of the mountain winter. This kind of movement is called altitudinal migration.

Mountain chickadees and bridled titmice are two mountain birds of the western United States. They often move down from high evergreen forests to spend winter in wooded valleys and streams.

The blue grouse, another resident of the western mountains, also changes altitude with the seasons. But this chickenlike bird does it in reverse. Before the mating season in spring, blue grouse move down from high mountain forests to open woodlands. There the males put on spectacular shows to attract a mate: They hoot, spread their tail feathers, and inflate the bright sacs on each side of their necks. Once the nesting season is over, the birds go back up the mountain.

Changing Diet with the Seasons

Some birds have special food habits that make it necessary for them to move south in winter. Nectar feeders, such as hummingbirds, must go where flowers are in bloom. Most insect eaters have to migrate to places where it is warm enough for insects to remain active throughout the winter. These include nighthawks, swifts, swallows, and some flycatchers, which feed by scooping up insects in midair, and most vireos and warblers, which pluck insect prey from the leaves and twigs of trees or shrubs.

But some insect eaters are able to stay in the North and find food even in the coldest weather. Carolina wrens, brown creepers, and most woodpeckers are expert in finding hibernating insects. They search beneath the scales of tree bark or within the wood itself for hidden eggs, pupae, and dormant adults.

Other year-round residents of the North can change their diets with the seasons. Like most birds, song sparrows and eastern dark-eyed juncos eat great numbers of insects in the warm months. In fact, insects make up about half their food in the summertime. But during winter they rely almost entirely on seeds from grasses and weeds.

In some cases winter means changing to a different menu. During spring and summer, blue grouse (see page 35) wander through the edges of mountain forests eating grasshoppers and other insects, wild berries, and the flowers, leaves, and buds of trees and low plants. In the high evergreen forests where they spend the winter, their main food is the needles of firs and other evergreen trees.

SUMMER FOOD | WINTER FOOD

song sparrow

junco

blue grouse

"SOMETIME" MIGRANTS

Most migratory species come and go on regular schedules and follow traditional pathways on their annual journeys. Irruptions are a different kind of seasonal mass movement. They occur when the supply and demand for food in the home territory get out of balance.

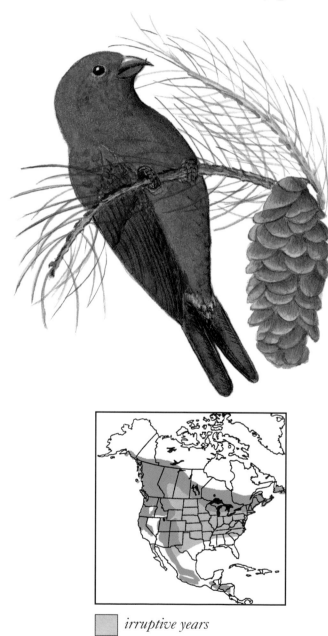

irruptive years

Irruptive species rely on a small number of foods for winter survival. Crossbills, for example, are finches that depend on the seeds of pine, spruce, and other evergreens for their food. They have unusual twisted bills, with tips that do not meet. Crossbills push their beaks between the scales of a cone to force them apart and then remove the hidden seed with their long tongues.

In some years the evergreen trees produce very few cones, causing a food shortage for the birds that depend on them. When this happens, the crossbills flood south in search of food.

The routes taken by irruptive birds seem to have no pattern. Evening grosbeaks banded (see page 44) in Pennsylvania one winter were found in seventeen states and four Canadian provinces in later years.

Snowy owls, like most irruptive species, are northerners. They live in the Arctic regions of North America, Europe, and Asia, where their main prey is the lemming, a small rodent of the Far North. About every four years the number of lemmings falls sharply.

The owl's normal winter range includes Canada, the northern rim of the United States, and the Great Lakes region. In winters when the lemming population is low, snowy owls move farther south to hunt rabbits, hares, ground squirrels, and other small rodents. In these irruption years some owls may wander all the way to California, Texas, Louisiana, Georgia, and even Bermuda.

irruptive years

Timing the Journey

Long-distance migrants make stressful journeys that may last for weeks. Before setting off, they wait for good weather and favorable winds that will make the trip easier. A mass of spring air moving up from the Gulf of Mexico may bring waves of migrants from the tropics to the United States. Weather also affects their progress during the journey. When hit by heavy rain or high winds, birds seek shelter and wait out the storm.

Some large, powerful birds, such as ducks, geese, and swans, fly rapidly and travel both night and day. They are able to cover great distances in a single flight.

tundra swan

But most kinds of birds making long migrations take to the skies in the night hours. Small land birds, such as warblers, thrushes, sparrows, wrens, and flycatchers—birds that normally are active only in daytime—migrate in the dark. They rest and feed all day and travel from twilight until dawn.

The long-distance travelers that fly in the daytime have special reasons for doing so. Swallows, swifts, and purple martins, for example, feed on flying insects and are able to eat while they travel. By evening they are well fed, and they use the night hours to rest for the next day's efforts. Soaring birds that use rising thermal air for their flights (see page 32) can migrate only by day. They must wait until

barn swallow

several hours after dawn before setting off on the day's journey.

Migrants do not move at the same speed at all times. In spring the birds hurry to reach their nesting grounds and begin raising young. In fall, when they are not driven by the urgency to begin nesting, the journey may take twice as long.

One way of measuring how long the journey takes is to capture banded birds (see page 44) at different points along their route. By measuring the distance traveled over several days, you can calculate the average daily progress. However, this method does not reveal the hourly flight speed because there is no way of knowing how many hours the bird has spent in the air. Some birds move steadily, while others make long stops to rest and feed. And in the spring migration some birds speed up as they come nearer to the nesting grounds.

Determining the actual flying speed of birds is tricky. Cars or airplanes that have kept pace with flying birds record some amazing speeds. A western pond duck, the cinnamon teal, was clocked at 59 miles (94 kilometers) per hour. A sandpiper, a small shorebird, *passed* an airplane that was traveling at 93 miles (150 kilometers) per hour.

cinnamon teal

But these are not normal speeds for birds. When they are being chased (by a car, a plane, or a predator) or when they themselves are in pursuit of prey, birds can double their regular speeds.

Radar guns used by traffic police to check speeding cars have shown that most migrant birds travel between 19 and 44 miles (30 to 70 kilometers) per hour, depending on the species and on the speed and direction of the wind.

STAY-AT-HOMES

About one-fifth of the 650 species of birds that nest in the United States and Canada do not migrate. Particularly in the southern states, where winters are mild and food is always available, more birds remain all year. Birds that stay in the same general area all through the year are called permanent residents.

Cactus wrens are residents of the southwestern deserts. They build nests and raise their young in cacti or in thorny trees and bushes. The wrens scratch in the leaf litter to find insects and spiders, and they also eat berries and seeds.

However, even the most severe places have some resident birds. The white-tailed ptarmigan (TAR-mi-gan) is a species of grouse that lives year-round in high meadows and windswept slopes where the weather is too harsh for trees to thrive. Ptarmigans always blend perfectly into their surroundings because they change their appearance with the seasons.

All birds grow new feathers at least once a year in a process called molting—old feathers fall out as new ones come in—but white-tailed ptarmigans molt three times yearly. In spring they are brown or black with a white belly, wings, and tail. The only bright color is a red comb above each eye. In summer some of the body feathers are replaced by new ones that are finely marked and speckled in brown and gray. The birds molt for a third time before the snows fall, becoming completely white.

Ptarmigans survive the frozen winter by eating the buds and twigs of shrub-size willows and birches.

Studying Migration

For centuries little was known about the winter homes of long-distance migrants. Bits and pieces of information came from travelers and explorers who reported seeing familiar birds in far-off places.

People tried to trace bird movements by marking individuals with ink or paint, but these marks disappear when the birds molt. Finally the use of numbered metal rings attached to the legs of captured birds, called banding or ringing, became the standard practice.

In North America bird banding is controlled by the United States Fish and Wildlife Service and by the Canadian Wildlife Service. These agencies issue the bands and receive records of all birds banded and of any bands that are recovered.

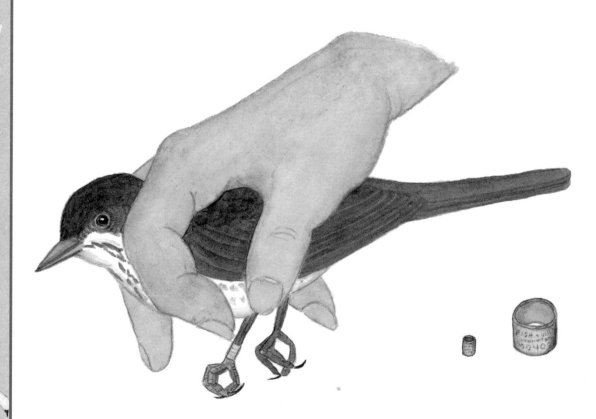

Bands come in different sizes for small and large birds.

Each band is printed with a serial number and the return address of the agency that issued it. After attaching the band, the bander notes its serial number; the bird's species, sex, and age; and the place and date of its capture. This information becomes part of the national database. Later reports of the bird—dead or alive—become part of the same record.

Bird banding pinpoints the bird's location at one fixed moment. In the last half century new technology has revealed more about actual movements. When migrating flocks fly across airport radar screens, radar can give the same information about them as it does about aircraft. It shows the numbers of birds and the direction, speed, and altitude of their flight. However, it cannot reveal the species of the birds.

Scientists can also follow a bird's movements by placing a miniature radio transmitter on its body. The tiny radio is either mounted on the bird's back in a harness or glued to a tail feather. Some birds carrying powerful transmitters have even been tracked by satellite.

A harness holds the transmitter and its antenna on the back of this gull.

WATCHING BIRDS
IN MIGRATION

With so many species on the move during spring and fall, these are wonderful times for watching birds. You will be able to see many species that are absent from your area at other seasons.

Any area of greenery may attract migrants when they set down to rest and feed during their journey. Check out your neighborhood parks and nearby forest preserves as well as lakes, shorelines, and other wetlands.

To identify the birds you see, you will need a pair of binoculars and a bird guidebook. The guides used by most birders are:

McCauley, Jane R. *Field Guide to the Birds of North America*, 2d ed. Washington, D.C.: National Geographic Society, 1993.

Peterson, Roger Tory. *A Field Guide to Eastern Birds*, rev. ed. Boston: Houghton Mifflin, 1980.

————. *A Field Guide to Western Birds*, rev. ed. Boston: Houghton Mifflin, 1984.

Robbins, Chandler, Bertel Brunn, and Herbert Zim. *Birds of North America*, rev. ed. New York: Golden Books, 1990.

The Peterson books may be best if you are a beginning birder. Since each volume deals with only a portion of the United States and Canada, it includes fewer species for you to consider when trying to identify a bird. However, the National Geographic and Robbins guides have a range map next to the description of each bird, so you can see at a glance whether it is likely to be in your area. (Peterson's excellent range maps are at the back of the books.)

The best way to learn about birds is to go out looking for them in the company of more experienced birders. Local bird groups—chapters of the National Audubon Society, the American Ornithologists' Union, and other bird or nature clubs—often have field trips that are open to the public. Members of such groups are also the best source of information about nearby birding hot spots.

You may have trouble finding these groups because they are usually run by volunteers and often have no offices. Your public library may receive their newsletters. Check those publications for contact names and telephone numbers.

If your family is planning a car trip, perhaps you can suggest a side visit to one of the national wildlife refuges. The United States Fish and Wildlife Service is responsible for almost four hundred refuges, many of them along migratory flyways. You can get information about them by writing to the regional office nearest to the area you will be visiting.

In Canada the network of national wildlife areas and migratory bird sanctuaries is run by the Canadian Wildlife Sevice. Private organizations, such as the National Audubon Society and The Nature Conservancy, also maintain refuges

The best reference book for locating birding sites in the United States and Canada is *Where the Birds Are*, by John Oliver Jones (New York: William Morrow, 1990). Organized by state, it lists national and private refuges, with instructions for visiting them, and tells you where to write or call for information about state refuges. It has charts showing which birds you can expect to see at the different national wildlife refuges and gives the names and addresses of many local birders' groups.

You can also find information about national refuges in the United States through the Internet. Go to the home page of the United States Fish and Wildlife Service at www.fws.gov/

Good birding!

INDEX

Page references to illustrations are in **bold**.